DO YOU WANT TO BE A DIGITAL ENTREPRENEUR?

What You Need to Know to Start and Protect Your Knowledge-Based Digital Business

Emmanuel Coffy, Esq. and Leonard Boyer, Esq.

Order this book online at www.trafford.com
or email orders@trafford.com

Most Trafford titles are also available at major online book retailers.

 www.trafford.com

North America & international
toll-free: 844 688 6899 (USA & Canada)
fax: 812 355 4082

Our mission is to efficiently provide the world's finest, most comprehensive book publishing service, enabling every author to experience success. To find out how to publish your book, your way, and have it available worldwide, visit us online at www.trafford.com

Because of the dynamic nature of the Internet, any web addresses or links contained in this book may have changed since publication and may no longer be valid. The views expressed in this work are solely those of the author and do not necessarily reflect the views of the publisher, and the publisher hereby disclaims any responsibility for them.

Any people depicted in stock imagery provided by Getty Images are models, and such images are being used for illustrative purposes only.
Certain stock imagery © Getty Images.

ISBN: 978-1-6987-1084-6 (sc)

ISBN: 978-1-6987-1083-9 (e)

Print information available on the last page.

Trafford rev. 01/27/2022

THE ENTREPRENEUR'S DIGITIAL SHIELD[SM]

BOYER COFFY ENTERPPRISES INC

Chapter I

Digital entrepreneurship is defined as creating new ventures and digitally transforming existing businesses by developing novel digital technologies and/or novel usage of such technologies. Digital products typically have very high profit margins and require no physical inventory.

The Fourth Industrial Revolution has rendered the concept of trading time for dollars obsolete and has transformed the main business engine into achieving financial prosperity through the concept of leverage, which is passive recurring income. This utilizes Evergreen Marketing, where something is done once but keeps on making money. You are no longer a worker, but a creative or business person. Money comes to you, without you constantly working for it.

In today's knowledge-driven economy, IP rights have become valuable business assets. Most successful companies in recent years have relied heavily on their creative and innovative capacity as their main source of competitiveness. Such inventiveness, know-how and creativity are captured and transformed into exclusive business assets through the acquisition of IP rights. This is why IP protection offers an important tool for businesses to enhance competitiveness and strengthen the position of their products or services in the marketplace.

"Intellectual property is the oil of the 21st century. Look at the richest men a hundred years ago; they all made their money extracting natural resources or moving them around. All today's richest men have made their money out of intellectual property." - Mark Getty

IP is the commodity and currency of the information age (the 21st century). For example, in 2016, Intellectual Property assets transactions accounted for more than twenty (20) percent of world trade, or approximately seven hundred forty ($740) billion US dollars. Compared to this amount today, just in the United States 52% of all U.S. merchandise exports is IP based or approximately 6.6 trillion dollars (38.2% of GDP). In the mid 70s, tangible assets made up approximately 80% of a company's value, with the remaining 20% in intangible assets. Today, intangible assets make up 84% of the value of a company and only 16% make up the tangible assets.

The rapid growth of IP coincides with the emergence of the digital economy, with the five largest companies by market cap changing too. In 1975 they were IBM, Exxon Mobil, P&G, GE and 3M. In 2018, they are Apple, Alphabet, Microsoft, Amazon and Facebook. Explosion of smart devices grew from 15 billion in 2015 to 200 billion in 2020 during that period.

Check out Airbnb, they are in the hospitality business. The company is valued at $105 Billion, but doesn't own one single house. How about Lyft valued at $15.68 billion and Uber valued at $75.11 billion? They are in the transportation business but do not own any cars. What do they own? Airbnb owns 191 patents, 58 trademark applications and other Intellectual Property (IPs). Lyft owns 618 patents; 36 trademark applications and Uber owns a total of 367 patents and 103 trademark applications and that's not all. This is simply an overview of their IP portfolios.

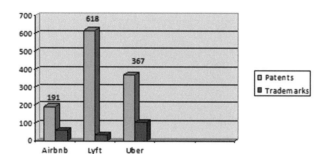

Some simple and cost-effective techniques can minimize the anxiety, yet help protect core assets.

To be a digital entrepreneur requires that you understand who it is you serve. Not everyone can be a digital entrepreneur. This is not a get-rich-quick scheme, nor will you make a lot of money in a very short period of time. But you must be willing to put in the work and do what no one else is willing to do for a period of time so that you can live the rest of your life the way you choose, and you can even become a digital nomad and work from anywhere like there is a laptop and an internet connection.

To be a digital entrepreneur requires you to focus on a specific group of people you wish to serve and provide real value to them, and it requires perseverance, focus, and discipline. You must be willing to continuously invest in yourself and try to improve whatever you do a little bit every day.

Digital entrepreneurs almost never realize that the most important way to succeed and protect what you are creating is utilize services of licensed attorneys and counselors-at-law. The attorney will set up the correct corporate entities and protect your intellectual property because failure to do so could cost you everything you worked so hard to achieve.

This e-book is designed to explain and help you understand certain legal concepts and how to utilize the legal system to protect you from potential catastrophe. This e-book is not designed to show you how to create a digital business, but we can recommend many excellent sources and tools to do so.

Contrary to popular belief, you must work on your strengths and hire a team to work on your weaknesses. In a famous interview of the legendary founder of the Ford Motor Company, Henry Ford was asked all sorts of questions pertaining to the automobile. He indicated that he did not have to know the answer; all he had to do was push a button (phones and dials and buttons in 1946), and the person who had expert knowledge would come in with the exact answer.

In this book, Boyer Coffy Enterprises Inc. will teach you about various types of corporate entities and explain which entities are the correct ones to utilize in your specific business. We will also explain to you how to properly protect your intellectual property. Remember, ignorance of the law is never a defense in a lawsuit or in life.

What follows below will be an explanation of various types of corporate entities that are available and which ones are best for your business and which ones should be avoided at all costs.

The purpose of the utilization of corporate entities includes, but is not limited to, protection against personal financial or other liabilities. There are also various tax advantages to the utilization of corporate entities, but analysis of that is beyond the scope of this book.

We begin this book with the discussion and explanation of the primary corporate entities commonly used by successful digital entrepreneurs and those that want to be successful. This will not include types of corporate entities that are rarely used by digital entrepreneurs.

The simplest type of business entity in New Jersey is called a *sole proprietorship*. There is no difference legally between the sole proprietor and the business owner because they are one and the same. There is no separation between the business and the person. Business income is considered to be personal, and there is no separate tax return that is filed for a sole proprietorship.

A sole proprietorship offers the owner no protection whatsoever from personal liability and therefore, in reality, serves no useful purpose. I would never encourage anyone to form a sole proprietorship.

The next type of business entity is called a general partnership. This has all the disadvantages of the sole proprietorship but multiplied by the number of partners in the general partnership. A partnership is defined as an association of two (2) or more owners and there are very few legal formalities required to form one. Although a partnership agreement is not legally required, however, it is a wise idea to have one custom drafted by a licensed attorney to meet the specific needs of the partnership. The partnership agreement will define the authority of each member of the partnership and the limits of what they can bind the partnership to without the consent of the other partners. Normally a partnership agreement is not filed with the State of New Jersey, however if a professional licensing Board or other regulatory agency requires partnership agreements to be filed with the State then that would have to be done.

It is strongly urged that a general partnership should have a custom drafted partnership agreement prepared by a licensed attorney, which among other things would establish the rights and obligations of each of the partners and establishes a managing partner. It could also specify what the obligations are of each partner and what they can and cannot do on their own.

This is for the protection of all members of the partnership and must have a precise wording and steps must be taken to ensure that this partnership agreement cannot be altered unless it is done with the consent of all the partners and an attorney custom drafting the revised partnership agreement.

The partnership operating agreement can also define under what circumstances a partner is allowed to sell their share of the partnership interest to an outside individual and it is highly recommended that the remaining original partners have the first right of refusal to buy out the partner who wishes to leave.

A general partnership does not protect the partners from personal liability for the acts of the partnership, and all the partners are jointly and severally liable for the acts of the partnership and all debts. The liability is personal, so therefore, improper actions or conduct by one of the partners can put all the partners and their personal assets at risk.

The other type of partnership is called a *limited partnership*. The limited partnership is very similar to the general partnership; however, it has a few significant differences. A limited partnership should definitely have a custom drafted partnership agreement by a licensed attorney. A limited partnership is managed by a general partner who also bears unlimited liability for the company's debts and obligations. A limited partnership also allows for any number of limited partners whose liability is limited to the total amount of their investment in the company.

A limited partnership's limited partners are frequently referred to as silent partners, which means that although they make investments in the company, they have no management over the day-to-day operations of the company, but they can be a valuable source of business capital.

A partnership agreement custom drafted by a licensed attorney should specifically set forth the powers of the general or managing partner and should specify whether or not any of the existing partners should have the right of first refusal prior to the sale of the shares of any limited partner to someone who is not a member of the partnership.

The limited partnership is frequently utilized by law, accounting, and financial firms, as well as various other types of professional service providers.

The first type of corporation is the *S or subchapter S corporation*. This corporation is the accountant's best friend but could be your worst nightmare. It requires far more accounting work than any other type of corporation other than a *C corporation* but has none of the advantages of a C corporation or, for that matter, an LLC, which is the *limited liability corporation*.

An S corporation has very limited liability protection for its owners. An S corporation does allow for perpetual existence and requires a corporate formation agreement, which lists the company directors, the officers, and the shareholders, as well as the employees of the corporation, and what their functions are.

Only US citizens and permanent residents can be owners of a subchapter S corporation. An S corporation may not have more than one hundred shareholders.

The company can issue shares of stock to investors, but most investors will not invest in any corporation that is not a C corporation.

Unless there is a properly drafted corporate operating agreement, which defines the management and operation of the corporation and its ownership, theoretically, any member of the subchapter S corporation can sell his or her ownership or his or her shares to anyone at random who may or may not be compatible with the rest of the ownership and management of the subchapter S corporation.

The income of the owners of a subchapter S corporation is reported to the IRS on the owner's personal income tax return, and the subchapter S corporation must also file a tax return.

Piercing the corporate veil of a subchapter S corporation is relatively easy, and that means the owners of the subchapter S corporation are also jointly and severally liable for any legal action brought against the subchapter S corporation and for any debts that it incurs.

There are many tax issues and formalities that are required of a subchapter S corporation, but those are beyond the scope of this book.

Absent extraordinary and unusual circumstances, the next two forms of corporations are the only ones that I would recommend to digital entrepreneurs.

A *limited liability corporation*, also known as an *LLC*, must use the term *LLC* in its name. An LLC must have an operating agreement that specifies the rights and obligations and names the managing member of the LLC. To be valid and to protect against piercing the corporate veil and having one's personal assets at risk, an LLC must have three members or more. An LLC does not require an owner to be a US citizen or permanent resident. Anyone can invest in an LLC, provided it is not some type of professional organization that requires a professional license and restricts ownership to members of that specific profession.

The owners of an LLC report their profits and losses on their own personal tax return. However, an LLC cannot issue shares of stock, but by being an LLC, it has enhanced credibility with other businesses, lending institutions, and the general public.

The next type of corporation, and the best, is a *C corporation*, which must have the abbreviation *Inc.* in its name. A C corporation is also complex to form and must have all corporate documents drafted by a licensed attorney. A C corporation can own multiple limited liability corporations. The C corporation is also considered the *gold standard of corporations*.

Contrary to popular misconceptions, a C corporation can be used by any type or size of business. Unless a specific state law or federal law prohibits it, a C corporation can issue an unlimited number of shares and other financial instruments, but a detailed discussion of this is beyond the scope of this book. The directors and officers of the C corporation have a fiduciary duty to the shareholders and employees of the corporation. With rare exceptions, a shareholder's liability in a C corporation is limited to the value of the shares of the corporation. A C corporation also has perpetual existence, and the original founding members of the corporation can all be deceased without the need of changing the corporate name.

The C corporation is held in the highest regard of any corporate entity by the general public, lending institutions, and potential and actual customers or clientele.

It is significant to note that once the company has Ten Million Dollars ($10 million) in assets and five hundred (500) shareholders, it is required to register with the SEC under the Securities Exchange Act of 1934.

A C corporation is subject to more oversight than other companies as a result of the tax rules and protection provided to the owners, who are not personally liable for any debts, lawsuits, or financial obligations.

You may be wondering why a digital entrepreneur would want to own both a C corporation and multiple limited liability corporations. There are numerous reasons for doing so, and a detailed discussion is beyond the scope of this book. For our purposes, a C corporation would be the primary business entity, and each LLC is separate and distinct from the C corporation and the other LLCs. By having both a C corporation and multiple limited liability corporations, each limited liability corporation should have one and only one business contained therein. This places two layers of corporate insulation between an individual and any legal or financial problems. Similarly, if one LLC is doing very well and the C corporation's ownership determines it is in the best interest of the C corporation to sell that LLC, they are free to do so without affecting the primary business of the C corporation or any other LLC. In the alternative, if the LLC is not working out, the LLC can file for bankruptcy, since it is a separate legal entity.

I cannot overstate the importance of having a licensed attorney custom draft all corporate documents, contracts, operating agreements, and other business documents. Numerous people have had to learn the hard way that using mass-market template-based services that purport to create legal entities or draft contracts often lead to serious personal legal and/or financial problems. Frequently, those can be totally prevented by documents custom drafted to that specific business's needs or the situation by a licensed attorney.

In our litigious society, it is often a wise idea to prevent problems before they occur by having the law firm on retainer that can be consulted with on a regular monthly basis with custom tailored legal advice and counseling plans. Sometimes these plans are called legal subscription plans and, depending upon the needs of the business, can be set at fixed price levels where certain amount of service is provided to the business for that month.

Digital entrepreneurs should have (among other documents) nondisclosure, noncompete, and noncircumvent contracts with people they employ either as gig workers, independent contractors, and even interns.

Digital entrepreneurs can prevent problems in advance from having contracts properly drafted that protect their rights and are in compliance with all applicable state and federal laws. This is not something that can be accomplished through the use of a template-based mass production service that purports to provide legal advice or documents, nor can this be done by a paralegal or other non-attorney.

If a digital entrepreneur has a law firm on a monthly retainer or subscription-based service, the business utilizes that law firm to review any contracts or other documents of significance prior to signing something that they may not understand. It is important to also realize that a court will construe any ambiguities in a contract against the drafter.

As the legendary football coach Vince Lombardi once famously said, "The best defense is a good offense." And countless people have stated that an ounce of prevention is worth a pound of cure. These may sound like antiquated colloquial terms, but they are just as valid and meaningful today as when they were originally stated.

Now in addition to having the right corporate structure, an extremely important element of being a digital entrepreneur and running a successful business is having your intellectual property (IP) properly protected. Attorney Emmanuel Coffy, Esq., is one of only forty-one thousand (41,000) members of the United States patent bar. Members of the patent bar are required to have a certain undergraduate degree prior to having a law degree and, after passing the state bar exam, must also sit for and take the patent bar exam, which means they have achieved a higher level of education and legal knowledge than a regular intellectual property attorney or any kind of non-attorney document preparer.

Chapter II

A digital entrepreneur is someone who is engaged in the on-demand or sharing economy made possible by technology-enabled platforms. This new era is referred to as the Fourth Industrial Revolution, and the great beneficiaries of this new trend are the providers of intellectual capital. Being a digital entrepreneur who is engaged in e-commerce using digital platforms, the marginal cost of producing each additional service (good) tends toward zero. If you fall within this category, you are invited to read on. As a result, you need to leverage your intellectual property (IP), which is the fuel of your enterprise. IP is the commodity and currency of the information age (the twenty-first century). For example, in 2016, intellectual property assets transactions accounted for more than 20 percent of world trade or approximately $740 billion. Compared to this amount today, just in the United States, 52 percent of all US merchandise exports is IP-based or approximately $6.6 trillion (38.2 percent of GDP). The rapid growth of IP coincides with the emergence of the digital economy, with the five largest companies by market cap changing too. In 1975, they were IBM, Exxon Mobil, P&G, GE, and 3M. In 2018, they are Apple, Alphabet, Microsoft, Amazon, and Facebook. Explosion of smart devices grew from $15 billion in 2015 to $200 billion in 2020 according to Intel. In the midseventies, tangible assets made up approximately 80 percent of a company's value, with the remaining 20 percent in intangible assets. Today, intangible assets make up 84 percent of the value of a company and only 16 percent make up the tangible assets.

Types of IP (Intellectual Property)

- **Patents. (process, machine, article of manufacture, composition of matter, design, plants)**
- Patents are the best protection you can get for a new product. A patent gives its inventor the right to prevent others from making, using, or selling the patented subject matter described in the patent's claims. The key issues in determining whether you can get a patent are: (1) Only the concrete embodiment of an idea, formula, or product is patentable; (2) the invention must be new or novel; (3) the invention must not have been patented or described in a printed publication previously; and (4) the invention must have some useful purpose. In the United States you obtain a patent from the U.S. Patent and Trademark Office, but this process can take several years and be complicated. You typically need a patent lawyer to draw up the patent application for you. The downside of patents is that they can be expensive to obtain and take several years,
- **Copyrights. (work of authorship fixed in tangible medium)**
- Copyrights cover original works of authorship, such as art, advertising copy, books, articles, music, movies, software, etc. A copyright gives the owner the exclusive right to make copies of the work and to prepare derivative works (such as sequels or revisions) based on the work.
- **Trademarks. (sound, device, symbol, word, phrase, brand name)**

- A trademark right protects the symbolic value of a word, name, symbol, or device that the trademark owner uses to identify or distinguish its goods from those of others. Some well-known trademarks include the Coca-Cola trademark, American Express trademark, and IBM trademark. You obtain rights to a trademark by actually using the mark in commerce. You don't need to register the mark to get rights to it, but federal registration does offer some advantages. You register a mark with the U.S. Patent and Trademark Office.
- **Service Marks.** Service marks resemble trademarks and are used to identify services.
- **Trade Secrets. (process, know-how, recipe)**
- Trade secrets can be a great asset for startups. They are cost effective and last for as long as the trade secret maintains its confidential status and derives value through its secrecy. A trade secret right allows the owner of the right to take action against anyone who breaches an agreement or confidential relationship, or who steals or uses other improper means to obtain secret information. Trade secrets can range from computer programs to customer lists to the formula for Coca-Cola.
- **Trade dress (various elements used to promote a product)**
- **Databases, customer lists**
- **Video/Audiovisual material**
- **B2B rights (use rights, broadcast rights, marketing rights, franchise agreements, royalty agreements, licensing agreements, sponsorship agreements, mortgage servicing rights**
- **Public rights (wireless spectrum rights, etc.)**
- **Brand Equity**
- **Rights of publicity (social media influencers)**
- **Traditional knowledge**
- **Confidentiality Agreements.** These are also referred to as Non-Disclosure Agreements or NDAs. The purpose of the agreement is to allow the holder of confidential information (such as a product or business idea) to share it with a third party. But then the third party is obligated to keep the information confidential and not use it whatsoever, unless allowed by the owner of the information. There are usually standard exceptions to the confidentiality obligations (such as if the information is already in the public domain).
- **Confidentiality Agreement for Employees and Consultants.** Every employee and consultant should be required to sign such an agreement, as discussed above.
- **Terms of Service and Privacy Policy.** If you are a company that conducts its business on the internet, it is important to have a terms of service agreement that limits what users can or cannot do on your website and with the information on your site. Closely related is your Privacy Policy, which sets forth what privacy protections are available to your users. The new European GDPR rules may also need to be addressed.

Most of your IP can be protected under one scheme of the law or another. Sometimes it is enough to protect your idea under only one of the schemes, but in other situations, it is best to protect your idea under several of these schemes. This is the idea of getting a bundle of rights to protect your ideas.

Many products out on the market are covered under several schemes of intellectual property, for example, patent and trademark. The patent protects a design, plant variety, process, machine, article of manufacture, or a compound. For example, the compound formula $C_8H_9NO_2$, which is known as acetaminophen, was protected by patent(s). These patents are now expired. Patents, you will find out, do have an expiration date, which is currently twenty years from filing. This formula, namely, $C_8H_9NO_2$, which is known as acetaminophen, may not mean anything to you but is an item that you are very familiar with by its trade name: Tylenol. This is an example of a trademark. While the patent has expired, any company with the capability to manufacture generic medicine can produce acetaminophen. In fact, there are many generics on the market. However, the trademark is still in force, and thus, the company who has the mark can still continue to generate revenue. There is no expiration date for a trademark. Therefore, if you have a good trademark, one that consumers like to buy, you can sell them forever and a day. Therefore, you want to protect your idea with a bundle of rights, here with a patent and a trademark. The patent allowed the owner to exclude all others from manufacturing the product for the time period the patent is in force while the product owner is promoting the brand. After the patent expired, the brand is well-known and will continue to protect the market share.

We envisaged six different scenarios for you to consider:

1. A digital entrepreneur who has an existing business with a domain name and trademark
   In light of the types of IP outlined above, you should review your IP portfolio consisting of the domain name and the trademark to formalize an IP strategy and determine how to augment your bundle of rights.

2. A digital entrepreneur who has an existing business with a domain name but no mark
   In this case, you should perform what's referred to as a knockoff search for your domain name to determine if you should consider trademarking the name. Again, you need an IP strategy based on your business goals and budget.

3. A digital entrepreneur who has an existing business with a trademark but no domain name
   In this case, as in every case, you need an IP strategy based on your business goals and budget. This approach applies to the remainder of the three categories.

4. A digital entrepreneur who is planning a new business with no name, mark, or domain name

5. A digital entrepreneur who has a new business with a name and a trademark but no domain name

6. A digital entrepreneur who has a new business with a name and domain

The foregoing scenarios and distinctions are premised on the fact that from 2003 to 2019, a total of 893,760 trademarks were registered by US companies and non-US residents, whereas the first quarter of 2020 closed with 366.8 million domain name registrations. Domain name registrations have grown by 14.9 million, or 4.2 percent, year over year.

If you are a digital entrepreneur who is planning a new business with no name, mark, or domain name, this section is for you. You should devote considerable time in choosing the name of your business. What's in a name? For starters, "naming" goes back to biblical times when God brought the animals to Adam to name the animals (Genesis 2:19). Some biblical commentators posit that having the man name the animals is another way of giving him responsibility to rule, subdue, and care for the animals. It is more than folklore to name something, someone. It is a significant and important milestone. Even more so today with the advent of the internet, which brings about domain names among other things.

As for the name of your business, it identifies the source of the goods and/or services you provide. It is better to choose a name that is arbitrary, with no direct relation to the associated goods or services. A name can become distinctive over time, thereby becoming a tremendous asset. For example, a Google search of RadioShack would reveal that "in May 2015, General Wireless Inc., an affiliate of Standard General, bought the company's assets, including the RadioShack brand name and related intellectual property, for US$26.2 million." Thus, it pays to invest the necessary time and intellectual resources to mastermind, conceive, and invent a name for your business. Ask yourself, What does Apple have to do with computers? But now Apple has acquired considerable "good will" and is famous. What does Xerox have to do with copying? I can go on and on. If an arbitrary name is unattainable or not desired, then the next best thing is to choose a name that is suggestive of the goods or services being provided.

Traditionally, naming an enterprise was always a difficult endeavor. It is even more difficult now. Sorry, life does not get easier. It has now taken a new dimension with the advent of the internet. In fact, today people talk about Industry 4.0 dubbed the new digital revolution, which ushers a new paradigm in the information age.

The reason is because you now have domain name added to the mix. In this day and age, you have your business name registered with one of the states; you also have a domain name for your website and trademark ideally with the federal government. Consequently, the best scenario is to have one name for the business as well as the domain name and the trademark. Why? Because your brand would be that much stronger if people don't have to scramble to recognize, remember, and recall your brand.

It is difficult to achieve though because of the fact that from 2003 to 2019, a total of 893,760 trademarks were registered by US companies and non-US residents, whereas the first quarter of 2020 closed with 366.8 million domain name registrations. Domain name registrations have grown by 14.9 million, or 4.2 percent, year over year. But the smart business person should want one name that resonates throughout. For example, Facebook, Uber, Lyft, Airbnb. You do not want one name for your business, another name for your domain name, and yet another name for your trademark.

It is not easy to achieve this feat. That's why we designed an algorithm using artificial intelligence (AI) to accomplish the task.

We are here to help. Contact us with your naming issues.

About the Authors

    I, Leonard Boyer, came of age in the '70s, the child of working-class union parents. I am a third-generation American and the first in my family to graduate law school and college half a year earlier than the normal time frame.

    As a young boy of ten, I quickly figured out that it was better to own a company than work for one, and that has never changed.

    I graduated with a dual degree in political science and psychology from the State University of New York at Buffalo after completing my education in three and a half years.

I had no real doubt that I wanted to be an attorney to be able to help me. Growing up, I watched many of the popular legal television shows of the time and read many books about famous attorneys.

After graduating early from college, I had an opportunity to work for a friend at his law office, who was a friend of the family, and so I could see the difference between working in a very small law firm. He also thought it was important for me to see what life would be like in a medium-sized law firm. It was a different way of practice, but in both firms, I learned about both the practice of law and the business of law prior to that phrase having its current meaning.

I had the privilege of being accepted into New York Law School in January 1980 and was one of just four people who completed the three-year law school early in two and a half years. I also had the advantage of knowing legal research and writing in a far more advanced way than my classmates.

Determined never to give up my dream of having my own law firm, I obtained employment in a few different types of law firms to provide myself with the experience and knowledge to learn about the day-to-day operations of a law firm and learn how to help more people.

I quickly learned how to make a difference in other people's lives, and I learned how to handle the emotionally charged situations for divorce and domestic violence and saw firsthand the difference a good attorney could make in people's lives. I mastered bankruptcy, mortgage foreclosure defense, mortgage loan modification, and so much more.

I successfully started several law firms over the course of my career, and in each one, I found more and more ways to make a difference in the lives of my clients, which I could see and they knew.

Today, together with my law partner Emmanuel Coffy, Esq., who is also a member of the patent bar, we have shown people how to benefit from Industry 4.0 and the knowledge revolution.

What you need to know about me and my law partner is that for us, some things have not changed over the years. We build relationships with our clients; we focus on helping them with their pains and their fears. Each client is still a name, not a file number.

Together, we offer aggressive, affordable professional representation. Now in these unprecedented very challenging times, we are ready to help you if you have the drive, determination, and passion to take full advantage of the knowledge revolution and Industry 4.0.

So do not let this pandemic play you. It's time to play the pandemic and let our firm help make your life better.

* * *

Emmanuel Coffy is a registered patent attorney and former patent examiner (www.coffylaw.com). Mr. Coffy is an inventor and had a long career as a digital design engineer. During his career as an engineer, he held positions such as lead design engineer. He supervised the US Air Force's largest network (Cape Canaveral, NASA) capable of supporting two simultaneous launches. His practice emphasizes patent application preparation, prosecution, and enforcement in the electronic arts, including business methods patents and design patents. Mr. Coffy has extensive experience in digital technologies, computer networks, and information technologies, as well as device physics, which includes semiconductor applications. Mr. Coffy coinvented a device called the low friction apparatus issued as US Patent No. 8,585,092. He also has experience in re-examination, litigation support, patent infringement assessment, patentability opinion letters, cease-and-desist letters, demand letters, and due diligence. Mr. Coffy also advises clients on intellectual property strategy, licensing, trademark, trade secret, copyright, and related unfair competition/deceptive advertising issues.

Practice Areas:

> Electrical/computer/software, telecommunications, mechanical, trademark and copyright, licensing, trade secrets and tech transfer, litigation and alternative dispute resolution infringement and validity analysis, trademark opposition/cancellation.

Admissions:

> He was admitted to practice law in the State of New Jersey, the United States District Court of New Jersey, the Court of Appeals for the Second Circuit, and the United States Patent and Trademark Office (USPTO).

Education:

> Juris Doctor (JD), Seton Hall University School of Law, Newark, New Jersey, 2003

> PhD, Candidate in Technology Management, Stevens Institute of Technology, 1998–1999

> MS, Electrical Engineering, Florida Institute of Technology, Melbourne, Florida, 1993

> BS, Electrical Engineering, Bridgeport Engineering Institute, Bridgeport, Connecticut, 1986

Publications/Speeches/Presentations:

> Coauthor of *The Value of Your Idea$* published by Trafford

> *The Need for Signal Claims* by Emmanuel Coffy and Albert Decady

> The Best Presenter Award, November 2011, by HABNET

Congressional Certificate of Special Recognition by Hon. Yvette Clarke, November 2011

New York City Council Citation by Councilman Matthieu Eugene, November 2011

New York City Council Citation by Councilman Jumaane D. Williams, November 2011

Presentation at the World Camp Academy, New York, 2017

Mr. Boyer and Mr. Coffy are the principals of Boyer Coffy Enterprises Inc., a Wyoming corporation that is dedicated to enable the digital entrepreneur's transformation into the realm of fresh thinking that creates wealth, thereby adding value to the business bottom line.

Printed in the United States
by Baker & Taylor Publisher Services